PEACE BE UPON US

PEACE BE UPON US
Poems by Iljas Baker

First published 2022 by Lote Tree Press
www.lotetreepress.com

Paperback ISBN 978-1-7398271-5-1
Hardback ISBN 978-1-7398271-4-4
e-book ISBN 978-1-7398271-6-8

© Iljas Baker 2022
All rights reserved

Designed by Maktaba
www.maktaba.co.uk

Cover image: Salaam (Peace) © Haji Noor Deen Mi Guang Jiang
www.hajinoordeen.com

The proceeds from this publication are donated to social programmes for children and the elderly in the Cambridge Muslim community.

A CIP catalogue record for this book is available from the British Library

بسم الله الرحمن الرحيم

In memory of my father (Robert Baker) and mother (Mary Baker)

Verily, in the creation of the heavens and the earth, and in the succession of night and day, there are indeed messages for all who are endowed with insight, [and] who remember God when they stand, and when they sit, and when they lie down to sleep, and [thus] reflect on the creation of the heavens and the earth: 'O our Sustainer! Thou hast not created [aught of] this without meaning and purpose.'

    Qur'ān 3: 190-191 (translated by Muhammad Asad)

Seek knowledge as far as China.

    Prophet Muhammad

I wonder at the man who observes the universe created by Allah but doubts Allah's Being and Existence.

    Hazrat Ali

The principal thing is the receptivity in the soul.

    Rumi

CONTENTS

ACKNOWLEDGEMENTS	13
PREFACE	15
ON BIG HEART MOUNTAIN	21
THE HIDDEN WORK OF BIRDS	31
A SOUND HEART AND WHAT COMES FROM HIM	34
SALAF (ANCESTORS)	38
A SUN ROSE	40
HOW TO THINK OF CANCER	42
A GOOD WORD	46
AFTER RAMADHAN	47
THE WIND CHIMES	48
IN MEMORY OF RADEN MAS BAPAK MUHAMMAD SUBUH SUMIHADIWIJOJO	49
SIGNS OF THE UNSEEN	50
SEEKING PERFECTION	57
THE REFUGES	58
WE LIVE PRECARIOUSLY	60

LIVING ON THE RIVER'S BANK	61
GRATITUDE	62
THEY ARE WHAT THEY ARE, WHATEVER THEY ARE	64
BODY AND MIND	70
YUSUF'S BEAUTY	72
THE PERFECT MAN	74
THE LAST CALIPH	76
THE CHILDREN OF YEMEN	78
REFUGEES	80
THE *SEMA*	82
IN MEMORY OF NOOR-UN-NISSA INAYAT KHAN (1914 – 1944)	84
FORESTS	86
TRUE STORIES	91
VEILS	93
GLOSSARY OF NON-ENGLISH TERMS	95

ACKNOWLEDGEMENTS

My thanks to the editors of the following publications in which some of the poems, sometimes in slightly different form, have appeared:

A Kaleidoscope of Stories: Muslim Voices in Contemporary Poetry, 2020 (Anthology) – "A good word"; "How to think of cancer"

Bosphorus Review of Books – "On big heart mountain" (July 2019); "The hidden work of birds" (September 2019); "The children of Yemen" (November 2019); "A sun rose" (March 2021)

Mediterranean Poetry – "The sema" (June 2020); "The last caliph" (July 2020)

Mostly Muslim (28 March 2020) – "Refuges"

Ribbons: The Journal of the American Tanka Society – "Seeking perfection" (Spring/Summer 2020)

Snapdragon: A Journal of Art and Healing – "Signs of the unseen, 2" (Fall 2020)

Soul-Lit: A Journal of Spiritual Poetry – "Yusuf's beauty" (Spring 2021)

We Humans 2020 (Anthology) – "The hidden work of birds, 3"

Thanks to Haji Noor Deen Mi Guang Jiang for permission to use some of his wonderful calligraphy. Haji Noor Deen was awarded the Certificate of Arabic Calligraphy in Egypt in 1997. He was the first Chinese person to do so. In 2017 he was awarded the Arabic Calligraphy Certificate in Istanbul, Turkey and is the first Chinese person to receive an ijazah in Ottoman calligraphy. His work has been exhibited throughout the world and has been acquired by many important institutions including The Asian Art Museum of San Francisco, The British Museum, The National Museum of Scotland and Harvard University Art Museums. His work can be found at www.hajinoordeen.com

PREFACE

I came to Islam through practicing the latihan kedjiwaan (spiritual exercise) of Subud, which I still practice and value for its role in my spiritual development. The spiritual exercise shaped my understanding of the need for and the role of Islam in my life and gradually opened up to me experiences of the ḥaqīqa (truth/reality) of Islam. For me, Islam, as expressed particularly in the Qurʾān and in those aḥādīth that don't contradict the Qurʾān, is guidance and support for living the present life while preparing for the life after death. This involves, above all, worshipping our Creator and the full expression of this worship goes beyond ritual worship and sharīʿa compliance to an engagement in the quest to realize the status of al-insān al-kāmil (the perfected human). Such a quest in the present era might seem fanciful, but the hope for abundant Divine Assistance makes it otherwise. This quest informs a number of the poems presented here as does my fondness for East Asian poetry.

I was attracted to Chinese and Japanese forms of poetry in translation over fifty years ago when I was a first-year undergraduate student in Glasgow. The attraction lay in their brevity, their sensitivity to nature, and their sense of the fragility and transience of life. Many of my favourite Chinese and Japanese poems also addressed the search for something beyond this life. Reflecting my growing interest in and practice of Buddhism I continued to explore Chinese and Japanese poets in translation throughout my undergraduate years and did so after I left Buddhism behind and even after I started following the teachings and practices of the Prophet Muhammad (peace be upon him) after completing postgraduate studies. I still enjoy these East Asian poems and they obviously influence some of my own poetry. Knowledgeable readers will easily recognize my debt to the poems attributed to the Chinese poet Han-shan (Tang era, 618–907), who, according to some scholars, may never actually have existed, or if he did he may only be one among a number of authors of the Han-shan corpus of over three hundred poems. Knowledgeable readers will also note my use of some Japanese poetic forms such as haiku, haibun and tanka, which for the most part have been adopted, and often adapted, to express a Muslim rather than a Buddhist worldview. Although I believe the two worldviews share much in common, I would never dismiss or diminish their differences; after all, it is their differences that played a large part in my embrace of Islam. The sensitivity to nature, and the sense of the fragility and transience of life have taken on new meaning in my own poems as a consequence of my practice and understanding of Islam and

Iljas Baker

I think this is obvious in many of the poems found in this brief collection. Apart from the East Asian poetry, I have found the "writings" of Jalāluddīn Rumi – the *Masnavī* (translated by Nicholson and by Gamard), the *Dīwān* (translated by Arberry) and *Fihi ma fihi* (translated by Thackston) – to be an important inspiration. The poems I have presented here are relatively short, simple poems that invite contemplation. The poems appear on a single page no matter how short they are. Hopefully this will help readers to refrain from moving on as quickly as possible to a new poem and encourage them to stay with the one they have just read and let it go beyond their surface mind and emotions. May these poems bring refreshment to hearts and minds. If a poem, a line or even a word should touch something deeper, I take no credit for that.

PEACE BE UPON US

Bismillah (In the name of Allāh). Image copyright of Haji Noor Deen Mi Guang Jiang

PEACE BE UPON US

Iljas Baker

ON BIG HEART MOUNTAIN

1

for as long as I can remember
I performed the obligatory prayers,
observed the fasts,
and did good works.
yet I remained unfulfilled.

when I set up home on big heart mountain
I let go of the self and its secret ambitions
to follow nature's way.
now when they ask how I am
I reply:
when the sun comes up the dew disappears

PEACE BE UPON US

2

when I lived in the town

I was forever rummaging in my past:

old lives

old loves

old losses.

no wonder progress was slow.

now I am on big heart mountain

with cool bright air

and surrounded by nature.

when people ask

who I am

I tell them with a smile:

I am a son of the moment

Iljas Baker

3

the townsfolk chatter about

the end of time.

it keeps them occupied

when work is scarce.

here on big heart mountain God is time -

no beginning

no end

PEACE BE UPON US

4

I remember when people

stayed at home.

now that the rulers are corrupt and cruel

everyone is on the move.

they're welcome to come to big heart mountain.

there's always work to be done,

simple food

and time to develop an aware spirit

Iljas Baker

5

if you avoid people

on big heart mountain

you will never get to know

your heart's contents

but if you want to develop

an aware spirit

be alive

when you're with the living

and be dead

when you're with the dead

PEACE BE UPON US

6

when I hear scholars

explain what an aware spirit is

my head spins

with their concepts and quotations

that lead further and further

from the heart of things.

I want to say:

honestly, what do *you* know?

Iljas Baker

7

I used to believe that

what is good is from God and

what is not good is from ourselves.

now that I've set up home on big heart mountain

I know it's true.

the signs are everywhere,

inside and

outside

PEACE BE UPON US

8

when giving in to your desires

has become a habit

you confine your Self to

narrow bitter paths

leading to suffering.

yet it's near impossible to change

this

unless you

replace it with something better,

like a dog giving up an old dry bone

for some fresh red meat

Iljas Baker

9

whether it's summer or winter

my voice croaks.

but still I chant the short sūrahs

and the ṣalawāt

as I wander these high winding paths

and narrow valleys.

my youthful self could never have imagined

this old man

praying for more time

to develop

an aware spirit

PEACE BE UPON US

Iljas Baker

THE HIDDEN WORK OF BIRDS

1

they traverse the firmament

guided by the stars

and an inner power

they bring us beauty and music

and signs

if we can read them

PEACE BE UPON US

2

mid-day birdcall

sudden, loud, insistent

penetrates the kitchen

where I'm standing

pulling *kaprao* leaves from their stems.

I'm startled

then I understand:

don't lose your Self in thought

Iljas Baker

3

(homage to 'Abd al-Qādir al-Jīlānī)

mixing the good fruit with the bad

is the only way to earn a living,

those market traders lie.

but the hoopoe says:

go directly to the orchard,

select only the good fruits

from the tree

and let the bad fruits fall

and rot

PEACE BE UPON US

A SOUND HEART AND WHAT COMES FROM HIM

aren't all poems entries in a travel journal recording and reflecting on the passing of states? the poet of Konya said *there exists outside of us a world for us to seek* and *the principal thing in man is in decline.* what to make of this? first quieten the disputatious mind. a simple hierarchy of souls or forces constitutes our life: material, vegetable, animal, human, perfect human and beyond these higher spiritual forces that reveal themselves to precious few. material forces dominate our lives. with increasing power and reach they shape our feelings and thoughts. they cause the *principal thing* in us to *decline*. we retreat into nature (a brief migration from overwhelming material to overwhelming vegetable and animal forces) and the profound contrast with our usual state leads us to mistake our

retreat for nearness to the Real.
nearness to the Real is not predicated
on place but on acquiring a sound heart
and on what comes from Him.

be aware of
    what He placed in you
        wherever you are

Iljas Baker

Lā ilāha illa Allāh. Muhammadun rasūlullāh. (There is no god but Allāh. Muhammad is the messenger of Allāh.
Image copyright of Haji Noor Deen Mi Guang Jian

PEACE BE UPON US

SALAF (ANCESTORS)

sacred   silence
not dreams recalled

not talk

revealed
the other lives
that bequeathed
what it was that
held them back

if we are shaped
by those who came before
whose then is this life of ours?

there is a life within this life
and through mercy and letting go
we can each become
our own true self

peace be upon us
on those who came before
and on those who will come after

Iljas Baker

seeing hope in
the life within this life

peace be upon us
through our own true self

no soul will bear another's burden
no soul will bear another's burden

PEACE BE UPON US

A SUN ROSE

there are so many stories
of that meeting
between Rumi and Shams
outside the sugar merchants' hostel
or in the courtyard
of some madrasa

Rumi fainted or he didn't faint
and Rumi's books
were consumed by fire
by water
or there were no books

but always the same question
posed by Shams

who was greater
Bayazid or Muhammad?

Bayazid spoke of being full of God
Muhammad admitted to being far from full

the answer seems obvious

Iljas Baker

but impossible.
a saint cannot be greater
than the Prophet.
impossible!
hence the fainting

then two images formed in Rumi's soul:
a cup in the rain quickly fills
and the ocean keeps receiving
that watery grace

Shams and Rumi became inseparable until
a sun rose within Rumi's soul

PEACE BE UPON US

HOW TO THINK OF CANCER

not as a battle but
as something coming
from the distant past
telling of the future

a lesson in threefold surrender.

say:

this is the forge
of the faith maker

Iljas Baker

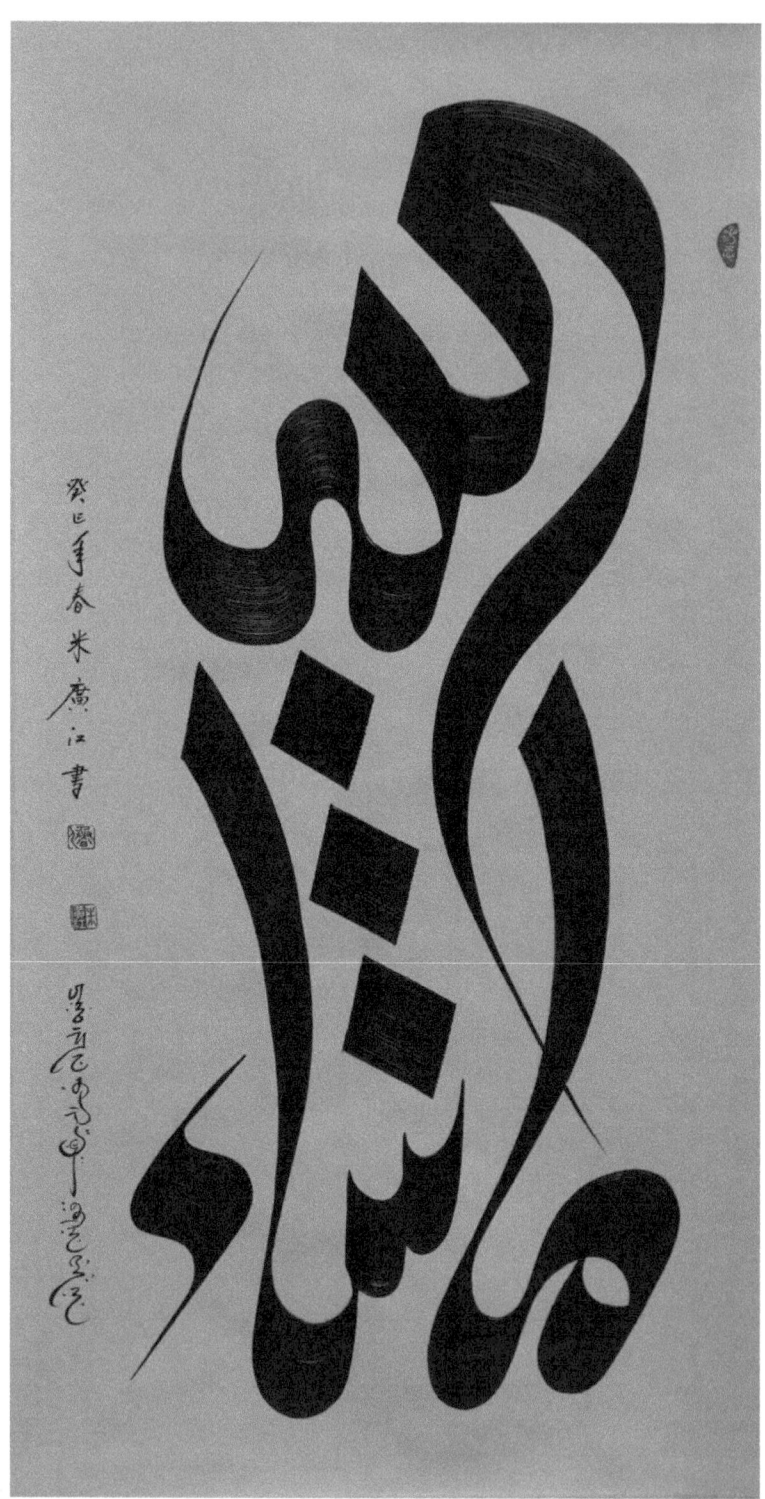

Iljas Baker

Masha'Allāh (Allāh's Will be done). Image copyright of Haji Noor Deen Mi Guang Jiang

PEACE BE UPON US

A GOOD WORD

you talked of trees
that morning
it was winter and the trees
were bare
it was cold outside

I said
(remembering Sūrah Ibrahim):
a good word is like
a good tree
with
firm roots
skyward branches
fruit bearing

later you almost wept
and inside I kept repeating
good words
Arabic words
and became firm
in faith in our mother's
winter journey from
this life to the next

Iljas Baker

AFTER RAMADHAN

the world rushes in
when you are not here
the placid lake where we sat in silence
becomes turbulent
I still awaken before dawn
though no drummer calls me
if anyone asks
how I am these days
I answer:

doesn't everyone feel at a loss for a time when Ramadhan ends?

PEACE BE UPON US

THE WIND CHIMES

the wind chimes' delicate tintinnabulations
come not from a snowclad mountain temple
but from my neighbour's yard
where the weekly washing is struggling to dry
on an old clothes horse

Iljas Baker

IN MEMORY OF RADEN MAS BAPAK MUHAMMAD SUBUH SUMIHADIWIJOJO

be joyful for

We loaned him to you

for a time

We gave him an elixir

and a golden tongue

so We could raise you

by degrees

and let you

taste eternity

be joyful and

thank him

call down Our blessings

on him

and stay

on his path

PEACE BE UPON US

SIGNS OF THE UNSEEN

1

one hundred birds sing

their invitation to prayer -

dawn's most precious gift

2

Indian cork trees

perfume my late evening walk –

vast sky, no thought

PEACE BE UPON US

3

shimmering lights float

on the river's still surface -

a tree cricket sings

Iljas Baker

4

last night's bright moon

faint now in the morning sky -

ah, this turning world

PEACE BE UPON US

5

see how time passes –

all are among the losers

except the *muslim*

Iljas Baker

6

vast sky full of stars

and the unceasing ocean

coming   and   going

PEACE BE UPON US

7

Indian cork trees

perfume my late evening walk –

vast sky, no self

Iljas Baker

SEEKING PERFECTION

adjusting a single white rose

in a clear glass vase

an old man

still tries

for perfection

PEACE BE UPON US

THE REFUGES

bismillāh I switch off the air conditioner and open the curtains and then roll up the blind. it's still dark. I listen to the birds singing and calling. They are not out in the numbers they will soon reach and the sounds have more silences between them than at other times. I listen for the virus and quietly recite an ancient prayer: "I take refuge in the Real from the Real". there is a world of understanding in that but modern humankind is resistant to it, resistant to what brings relief but not to most of what threatens its well-being. later I walk my usual route around the community where I live. there's a slight breeze that cools me and I walk faster. I turn into a narrower road that leads to the lanes where most of the houses are. suddenly I stop. in front of me is a golden shower tree with a profusion of intense yellow blossoms.

Iljas Baker

I'm filled with wonder and gratitude. the tree is in a garden at the mouth of a lane and its branches hang over onto the road. many of the trumpet-shaped flowers will eventually fall there. soon they'll fade before or after the road sweepers do their work

golden shower tree
    flowers effulgent -
        its secret fully revealed

PEACE BE UPON US

WE LIVE PRECARIOUSLY

we live precariously

between two fires

yet secure enough

and with

time enough

to gaze on

the beautiful

and reflect

Iljas Baker

LIVING ON THE RIVER'S BANK

living on the river's bank

you are always near the river

when you are thirsty

you can drink

when you are hungry

you can find food

when you are hot

you can cool yourself

when it's necessary

you can cleanse yourself.

when will you move there?

the best thing you will ever do is move there

PEACE BE UPON US

GRATITUDE

I awaken, sit on the edge of the bed and sip some water from a glass that I keep on the bedside table. the birds have started singing and calling. I listen for a while but it's hard to detect a pattern as they seem to sing and call without reference to each other and some sing or call loudly whereas others do so softly. I go to the bathroom and do my ablutions and then return and perform the morning prayer. by the time I'm finished the birds appear to have thinned out. the mynah bird with its raucous call has certainly gone or has become silent. when it's light I go for a walk round the community where I live. the sun is low in the sky and its light is not harsh. there's something almost tender about it easing us into the day after the long night. there are many mangrove trumpet trees and various kinds of jasmine trees lining the roads and most gardens have a variety of trees as well as leafy plants and flowers. as I turn on to a shorter road I notice that numerous large white flowers have fallen from the mangrove trumpet trees onto the road creating an intriguing pattern. as I contemplate God's land art I can't help but exclaim *al-ḥamdu li-llāh, al-ḥamdu li-llāh, al-ḥamdu li-llāh* and my mind and feelings expand enlarging my world

flowers bloom in the night
    and fall before sunrise -
        surely not just for me

PEACE BE UPON US

THEY ARE WHAT THEY ARE, WHATEVER THEY ARE

FAITH

faith

is the letting go

of cleverness

to receive

wisdom

Iljas Baker

REMEMBRANCE

remembrance

of God

is

faith's

anchor

PEACE BE UPON US

PATIENCE

patience

is rooted

in time

but bears fruit

in

timelessness

Iljas Baker

SERVANTHOOD

accepting

the limitations

of time and space

is part

of servanthood

PEACE BE UPON US

LIVELIHOODS

God made us

needy

so we

could have

livelihoods

Iljas Baker

SOUL

what sustains us on

this path

is

soul

fulness

not

mindfulness

PEACE BE UPON US

BODY AND MIND

bismillāh I leave the central plain where I live and head northwest passing along the Sankampaeng mountain range. my feelings of homesickness which I experience infrequently are assuaged. when I arrive at my destination my host brings cherry juice that has just been prepared using cherries from the wild garden that lies at the base of a well-forested hill. the juice is sour but it is full of vitamin c and that is reason enough to drink it and even accept a refill. the juice was made from a type of cherry called mountain cherry or wild Himalayan cherry. although it looks like a cherry it doesn't have a stone in the middle and therefore technically it is a berry and not a fruit. later my host gives me an abundance of mangoes, the type that is particularly good with sweet sticky rice and coconut cream. I am also given bunches of mint that I will plant in my garden and a large

Iljas Baker

container of dried rose petals most of which I will use for tea or cold water infusions and some of which I will use for my bath (like the Javanese) after the beginning of Ramadhan is announced in a few days' time

body and mind
    are nourished by
        the earth's abundance

PEACE BE UPON US

YUSUF'S BEAUTY

the light diminishes

and there is a faint rumbling

in the darkening sky.

suddenly there is a new and different light,

this time coming from Yusuf.

Zuleikha's ladies were paring and cutting

apples and pomegranates

when he entered.

all were awed by his beauty.

some fainted,

the rest were speechless,

the fruits fell from their fingers

on to their robes

on to the carpets

and they were cutting themselves.

Iljas Baker

absorbed in his beauty

they felt no pain

in their bloodied hands.

could our deaths be like this,

light and beauty

indistinguishable

calling us free

from what we have no need of?

the pain is someone else's,

the light, the beauty growing

growing

PEACE BE UPON US

THE PERFECT MAN

every time I make this journey to the cancer hospital the traffic is dense especially when I am close to the railway lines that transect a very busy crossroads. fortunately the hospital grounds have numerous trees and plants so there is an immediate feeling of relief when I arrive despite my reason for coming. there used to be more trees and plants but many of them were cleared to create more parking spaces. the hospital's services are in greater demand these days and I've noticed that many patients are young. this wasn't so when I started coming here seven years ago. I have to park my car some distance away from the building where I have an appointment. thankfully the sun is shining with a quality of light that seems to bless everything and everyone. usually a prayer in English or Arabic, is on my lips. the hospital was founded by and named after one of the Thai princesses. the doctors and nurses as far as I can tell are Buddhists and much of the reading material in the waiting rooms is about Buddhism. I respect it but I don't read it. just before I reach the building where the mri will take place I pass an almost life size statue of the Buddha depicting his enlightenment. his right hand is touching the ground which is known as the *bhumisparsha mudra* symbolizing asking the earth to witness the reality and solidity of his triumph over Mara, the personification of his *nafs*. his left hand is resting on his knee palm upward symbolizing receptivity. it doesn't feel alien to me this Buddha, this symbol of human perfection. peace be upon you al-*insān al-kāmil* I say quietly as I pass

the perfect man knows
  the self-deception of inaction
    and the limitations of his own actions

PEACE BE UPON US

THE LAST CALIPH

this is what will happen now
they told him that spring night
briefly interrupting
his reading of Montaigne.

he placed his finger on the page
and looked up coldly.

greatness of soul is knowing
how to circumscribe and set oneself in order
he read when alone again.

this is what will happen now
they told him that spring night,
the past is dead
truth and justice will be better served.

In the morning a final *fajr*

Iljas Baker

a brief *zikr* and then exile.

two wives three children one grandchild
waited anxiously downstairs by the cars
slowly and sadly they left the Dolmabahçe palace,

they followed the curve of the Bosphorus,
crossed the Galata bridge,
passed the mosque of Beyazit
and went through the Edirne gate.

at Çatalca the not yet fabled Orient Express
was waiting to take them to Europe

there the last caliph
read Montaigne
and the Qur'ān
wearing a fez

PEACE BE UPON US

THE CHILDREN OF YEMEN

we talk in whispered

broken San'ani sentences

never fully present

waiting

watching

anxiously

we believe

but our hearts fear

the future

we might be gone

our children gone with us

would be a blessing

their broken bodies

still with life

unbearable

we believe

but our hearts fear

the future

Iljas Baker

don't ask too much of us

O Compassionate

O Merciful

we believe

but our hearts fear

for our children's future

PEACE BE UPON US

REFUGEES

they did not start the wars

and they will not end them

they did not set the world ablaze

and they will not extinguish it

they are small

like you and me

they are fleeing with what is left

of lives

broken then crushed

they are fleeing from dying too soon

crossing lands and seas

the children slow them down

but they don't complain

traveling with strangers

they never think of how they look

Iljas Baker

they still share

show gratitude

nourish hope

one day

we will need them

PEACE BE UPON US

THE *SEMA*

forty years ago

Istanbul seemed larger

it was the same *sema*

perfectly symmetrical

cosmically significant

in ancient times a prayer now a performance

what once was spontaneous was perfectly orchestrated

and there was a clock on the wall

no question of the *semazens'* longing being fulfilled

there was no longing

no need to hide their ecstasy

there was no ecstasy

but it was perfect art

and everyone was happy

later I drank Turkish coffee

and ate baklava stuffed with pistachios

Iljas Baker

somewhere in Fatih

and contemplated

that moment at the commencement of the *sema*

when the dervishes loudly slapped the floor in unison

PEACE BE UPON US

IN MEMORY OF NOOR-UN-NISSA INAYAT KHAN (1914 – 1944)

too delicate for war they said

yet war's victims freighted her soul

and defiance took root there

Krishna and Arjuna (not Ali) inspired her

the Mahākapi Jātaka helped her persevere

her soft high-pitched voice

only rarely broke through silence

to speak of mundane things

and sacred things

and the joy brought by sacrifice

was there joy Noor

in the neat houses and walled gardens of Suresnes?

in the damp crowded quarters of England?

Iljas Baker

in the dangerous streets and secret rooming houses of Paris?

in the cold prisons of Karlsruhe and Pforzheim?

in Dachau?

did joy retreat Noor

was it hidden from you

until finally it gave way

to a greater joy?

PEACE BE UPON US

FORESTS

1

I left the city

tired of making plans

to find rest for a time

where capercaillie

goldeneye

and siskin nest

rain fell fitfully most days

but still I wandered there

until recent memory was erased

and thought cleaved to what was in front of me

what was it I felt

in the body

Iljas Baker

in the blood

and in the clear bright mind?

it was something like *dhikr*

PEACE BE UPON US

2

when night fell

only the soft light

of the northern stars

illuminated the forest's interior

wearily I eased my body into

the undergrowth of

mosses and lichens

and slept for a time

suddenly I was awakened

by a moving shape

coming closer

closer

a red deer

stopped abruptly

Iljas Baker

then turned and fled

and I listened until its sounds faded

my fear diminished

and only awe remained

PEACE BE UPON US

3

we trekked all day

through the warm humid forest

then after dark

came across a clearing

good enough for rough sleeping

exalted and exhausted

we readied our places

then silence

reigned

for a while

and dreamscapes

in multiple languages

were all we knew

Iljas Baker

TRUE STORIES

(for Ken Mellin)

stories sought him out.

it's obvious now

when so many stories are waiting to be told

what happens to untold stories

is the same as what happens to unpicked fruit I imagine

the ancients said a fruit reaches its heaven when eaten

by a true human

so perhaps a story reaches its heaven when told

in truly human company

the last story he told me was

as many were

fascinating but improbable

about a fateful meeting between an animal

and some humans

PEACE BE UPON US

about life and death

and our illusions no less

at the end I was waiting for him to laugh and say I made that up

but he didn't because it was a true story

let the first untold story you find be told in his memory

Iljas Baker

VEILS

on a late evening walk
to still
the wheel of thought
the sweet spicy scent
of tree jasmine
the sound of
water falling
a bright crescent moon
and a shining star
are all laid out before me
and behind these wondrous veils
are the many Names of God

PEACE BE UPON US

Iljas Baker

GLOSSARY OF NON-ENGLISH TERMS

Aḥādīth	Collected reports of the sayings or practices of Prophet Muhammad (sing. *ḥādīth*)
al-ḥamdu li-llāh	Praise be to God
al-insān al-kāmil	Perfect human. The highest stage a person can reach, but only with Divine Assistance
bhumisparsha mudra	"earth-witnessing" hand gesture of the Buddha
bismillāh	In the Name of Allāh. This is said by Muslims at the start of any activity
dhikr	Remembrance. A form of Divine worship involving repetition of certain Arabic

	words or phrases , e.g. *Allāh* or *lā ilāha illallāh*. It can be done alone or in a group and may involve rhythmic chanting and movements. It can also refer to maintaining the feeling or awareness of the presence of the Power of God in one's soul
haibun	A Japanese form of poetic expression combining a prose poem and a *haiku*
haiku	A short form of poetry originating in Japan. Most *haiku* focus on nature and have a reference to a specific season. Traditional *haiku* written in or translated into English generally consist of three lines in a 5-7-5 syllabic pattern (in imitation of the pattern found in Japanese *haiku*) but modern *haiku* (for better or worse)

	tend to eschew tradition partially or entirely
ḥaqīqa	Truth, reality - as perceived by the eyes of the soul
ijazah	Permission or authorization to teach
latihan kedjiwaan	Spontaneous spiritual exercise based on surrender to the Power of God. The sustained practice of the exercise results in purification of the soul and inner guidance in all aspects of one's life. Men and women do the exercise separately. There are no shaykhs or teachings involved. It is available to people of any religion and none
muslim	Those who surrender to the One God and do good deeds whatever their professed religion

nafs	The word *nafs* has a number of meanings but it is often used to refer to the ego, the lower self, the passions
ṣalawāt	Prayer asking God to bless Prophet Muhammad and his family
sema	A form of Divine worship involving music and movement. The best known is the *sema* of the Mevlevi Dervishes
semazens	Those performing the *sema*
shari'a (often written as shariah)	The righteous path or God's path. The entire normative system of Islam. To be distinguished from *fiqh*, which is the Islamic legal system derived from *shari'a*
Sūrahs	Chapters of the Qur'ān

tanka	Another poetic form of Japanese origin. When written in English it tends to consist of 5 lines in a 5-7-5-7-7 pattern (imitating the Japanese pattern). Modern writers of *tanka* in English often eschew traditional characteristics

PEACE BE UPON US

Iljas Baker

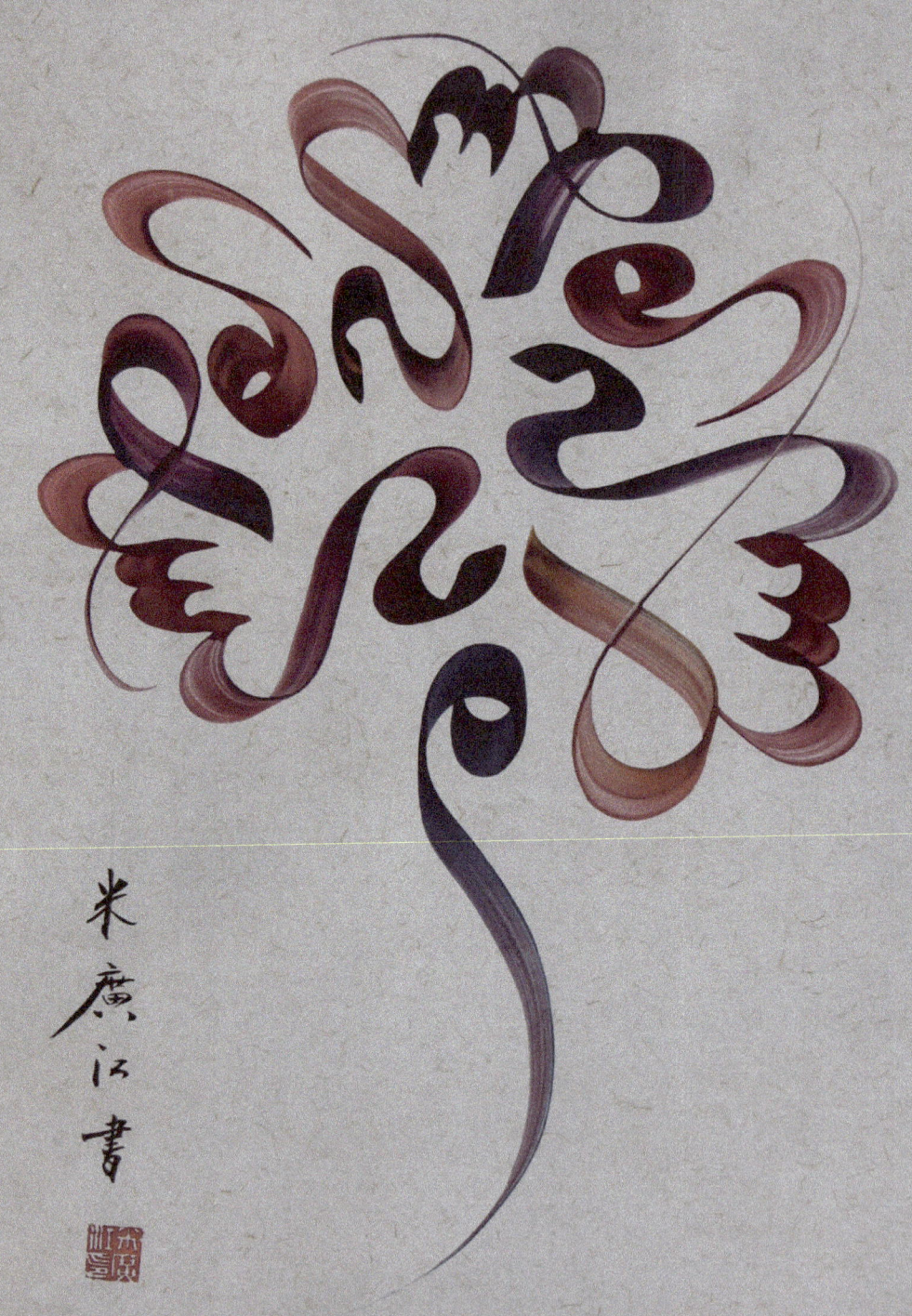

Iljas Baker

Salaam (Peace) Image copyright of Haji Noor Deen Mi Guang Jiang

PEACE BE UPON US

Iljas Baker

Also from Lote Tree Press

A Kaleidoscope of Stories:
Muslim Voices in Contemporary Poetry

Symphonies of Theophanies:
Moroccan Meditations
by Peter Dziedzic

All the Birds were Invited to a Feast in the Sky
by Soukeyna Osei-Bonsu

From This Street to the Moon
By Nabila Jameel

The Well at the Desert's Heart:
Verses of Healing
by Tony Bowland

Light Steps:
A Poem on the Seerah of Prophet Muhammad ﷺ
By Ali Scully

www.ingramcontent.com/pod-product-compliance
Lightning Source LLC
LaVergne TN
LVHW072021060526
838200LV00023B/391/J